MANHATTAN MEMORIES

A BOOK OF POSTCARDS OF OLD NEW YORK ☒ MUSEUM OF THE CITY OF NEW YORK

Pomegranate

SAN FRANCISCO

Pomegranate Communications, Inc.
Box 6099, Rohnert Park, CA 94927
800-227-1428
www.pomegranate.com

Pomegranate Europe Ltd.
Fullbridge House, Fullbridge
Maldon, Essex CM9 4LE
England

ISBN 0-7649-1368-9
Pomegranate Catalog No. A994

Pomegranate publishes books of
postcards on a wide range of subjects.
Please contact the publisher for more information.

Cover designed by Lisa Reid
Printed in China
09 08 07 06 05 04 03 02 01 00   10 9 8 7 6 5 4 3 2 1

To facilitate detachment of the postcards from this book, fold each card along its perforation line before tearing.

From the old Polo Grounds and Ebbetts Field ballparks to the once-ubiquitous Woolworth's lunch counters and Automats, *Manhattan Memories* elicits a familiar fondness for things past. Drawn mostly from the Museum of the City of New York's rich photographic archive, this collection includes work by renowned photographers Berenice Abbott, Jacob Riis, and Andreas Feininger, along with the strong imagery of prolific commercial firms—including the Byron Company and the Wurts Brothers—whose collections at the museum form an unparalleled documentary resource. Complementing these selections are several evocative photographs representing the work of lesser-known or unidentified artists—a staple of the museum's remarkable archive of New York City images.

The Museum of the City of New York's collections—numbering some 1.5 million objects—cover a diverse range of subject matter. These vintage images, a cherished part of the collections, celebrate both iconic and lesser-known New York City phenomena—all now extinct—and ask, "What will tomorrow's memories of New York City be?" Whatever the answer, the Museum of the City of New York is sure to be on hand with artifacts and images that tell the stories of this vibrant and always-changing metropolis.

—*Peter Simmons*
Deputy Director for Exhibitions, Publications,
and Electronic Media, Museum of the City of New York

CENTRAL PARK
BULL-FIGHT
ARENA.

Cor 116th St. & Sixth Ave.

Between the Two Stations of the Third and Sixth Avenue Elevated Railroads.

The Celebrated (Toreros) Spanish Bull-Fighters will give

3 GRAND BULL-FIGHT

PERFORMANCES ONLY.

On SAT, JULY 31st,

WED. AUGUST 3d and SAT. AUGUST 6th.

Three Grand Bull Fights will be given by a first-class company of Spanish Bull-fighters under the direction of the

Espada—Angel Valdemoro,

This professional has been very successful in all his performance, and was one of the three chiefs who took part in the bull-fights, given on the occasion to the throne of Spain of the present King Alfonso XII. He was also leader in the Royal bull-fights which took place at the marriage of said King.

All the artists are among the most celebrated and applauded in all the Spanish cities, and they will play most difficult and risky feats with the bulls, avoiding the rage of the animals by their great skilled intelligence with the aid of the CAPAS.

NO FIGHT will be had, causing any injury to the animals, only taking teams of the PICADORES.

The spectacle will be very exciting and extremely agreeable, for all the persons who will go to these performances.

A Large Arena has been built at great expense, expressly to accommodate and give to the performance the required splendor.

SIX WILD TEXAS BULLS !!!

Will perform. In case of one not being wild enough, it will be replaced by another bolder or more excellent qualities for this sort of amusement.

The bulls will be from Texas, as the fights in Havana have shown that the spirited qualities of the Texas wild bulls are of the best.

The sale of Tickets will commence Tuesday 27th inst. at the above places Tickets will be open at the said offices for any of the three performances at the demand will be so great that it will be impossible to accommodate all at the first performance.

| General Admission $1.50. | Seats in Amphitheatre 50c. |
| Seats on First and Second Rows $1. | Private Box (6 chairs) $12. |

Children Under 8 Years Half-Price.

Doors Open at 3. Performance to Commence at 3 P. M.

A First-Class Band has been engaged for the occasion.

ANGEL FERNANDEZ,

84 Oliver Place, New York.

Charles Lazus, Printer, 84 Oliver Place, New York.

MANHATTAN MEMORIES

Bullfight, Central Park Arena, July 31, 1880
Broadside
Gift of E. P. Chrystie

Situated at the corner of West 116th Street and Lenox Avenue, just north of Central Park, New York's only bullring was erected in 1880 and seated 10,000 spectators. This broadside advertises the bullfights to be "very exciting and extremely agreeable for the ladies."

BOX 6099 ROHNERT PARK CA 94927

Pomegranate

MANHATTAN MEMORIES

American Theatre Roof Garden, 1898
Silver gelatin print
The Byron Collection

Theater roof gardens became popular in the early 1880s and
flourished into the 1920s, when Prohibition and interior cooling
systems rendered them obsolete. The American Theatre Roof
Garden opened on June 19, 1893.

BOX 6099   ROHNERT PARK   CA 94927

Pomegranate

MANHATTAN MEMORIES

Pennsylvania Station, n.d.
Silver gelatin print

Still remembered fondly by scores of New Yorkers, McKim, Mead
& White's extraordinary Pennsylvania Station provided a grand
entrance to the City. Its demolition in 1963 was vehemently
protested and led to the 1965 formation of the New York City
Landmarks Preservation Commission.

BOX 6099   ROHNERT PARK   CA 94927

Pomegranate

MANHATTAN MEMORIES

Madison Square Garden, c. 1900
Silver gelatin print
The McKim, Mead & White Collection

Designed by renowned architect Stanford White, old Madison
Square Garden (1890) included an amphitheater, concert hall,
theater, roof garden, and restaurant. Ironically, White was fatally
shot on the roof garden by the jealous husband of showgirl Evelyn
Nesbit, White's former mistress. It was demolished in 1925.

BOX 6099 ROHNERT PARK CA 94927

Pomegranate

MANHATTAN MEMORIES

Fifth Avenue Bus, Washington Square, October 21, 1936
Berenice Abbott
Silver gelatin print

In 1907, the Fifth Avenue Coach Company began replacing horse-drawn coaches with the double-decker motorized buses that would become a trademark of the company. When Washington Square Park was redesigned in 1966, buses were rerouted outside the park's confines.

BOX 6099   ROHNERT PARK   CA 94927

Pomegranate

MANHATTAN MEMORIES

Elevated Railroad Station, Third Avenue and 59th Street,
c. 1910
Silver gelatin print

Elevated railroads continue to define the character of several New York City neighborhoods. However, most of the Manhattan "Els" were demolished in the 1940s and 1950s. The Third Avenue El, shown here at the 59th Street, or "Bloomingdale's," station, came down in 1955.

BOX 6099   ROHNERT PARK   CA 94927

Pomegranate

MANHATTAN MEMORIES

Third Avenue El Train Near 10th Street, n.d.
Silver gelatin print
J. Clarence Davies Collection

Before the electrification of the elevated railroads, steam locomotives
pulled the wooden passenger cars.

BOX 6099 ROHNERT PARK CA 94927

Pomegranate

COPYRIGHT 1896 BY J.S. JOHNSTON, N.Y.

MANHATTAN MEMORIES

The Old Post Office, 1894
J. S. Johnston
Silver gelatin print

This elaborately colonnaded, mansard-roofed U.S. post office,
situated at the triangular tip of City Hall Park, opened in 1878 to
a barrage of negative reviews. The building was demolished in
1938, when beautification of City Hall Park for the 1939 New
York World's Fair hastened its demise.

BOX 6099   BOHNERT PARK   CA 94927

Pomegranate

MANHATTAN MEMORIES

Checker Marathon Taxicab, 1980
Checker Motor Company
Gift of Dr. Gerald Rosen

Gasoline-powered taxicabs became a popular mode of transportation in the City in 1907, replacing horse-drawn hansom cabs and slow-moving battery-powered vehicles. In 1967, the City ordered all medallion taxicabs to be painted the now-familiar bright yellow. Roomy Checker cabs were popular in the 1950s and 1960s, and they remained on the streets until 1999.

BOX 6099   ROHNERT PARK   CA 94927

Pomegranate

MANHATTAN MEMORIES

The Sheep's Meadow, Central Park, c. 1880
Silver gelatin print

Sheep grazed on Central Park's Sheep Meadow until 1934, when
they were banished by a reforming administration, claiming that
the sheep were inbred and produced malformed progeny.

BOX 6099   ROHNERT PARK   CA 94927

Pomegranate

MANHATTAN MEMORIES

Mullin's Alley, Cherry Hill, c. 1890
Glass lantern slide
The Jacob A. Riis Collection

Journalist and social reformer Jacob A. Riis photographed the
slums of the Lower East Side in an effort to publicize the cause of
their inhabitants. His photographs have become symbolic of New
York City's notorious turn-of-the-century tenement life.

BOX 6099   ROHNERT PARK   CA 94927

Pomegranate

MANHATTAN MEMORIES

Bird's-Eye View of the New York Crystal Palace and Environs, 1853
John Bachman
Hand-colored lithograph
J. Clarence Davies Collection

The New York Crystal Palace was erected in 1852 on the site of what is now Bryant Park as an exhibition hall for the United States' first World's Fair. The "fireproof" iron-and-glass structure burned to the ground in 1858.

BOX 6099   ROHNERT PARK   CA 94927

Pomegranate

MANHATTAN MEMORIES

Last Horsecar in New York City, July 26, 1917
Silver gelatin print

The world's first horsecars began in New York City in 1832. The mode of
transportation was gradually replaced, beginning in the 1880s, by cable cars.
New York's last horsecar ride, depicted here, began at the intersection of
Broadway and Bleecker Street on the morning of July 26, 1917.

CA 94927

ROHNERT PARK

BOX 6099

Pomegranate

MANHATTAN MEMORIES

The Empire State Building, December 16, 1930
Robert A. Knudtsen
Silver gelatin print
Gift of Mr. Robert A. Knudtsen

The 200-foot spire of the Empire State Building was designed as a mooring mast for zeppelins. But the designers failed to take into account the power of high winds, and the plan was never fully realized. This juxtaposition of a U.S. J4 airship with the mooring mast under construction provides a vision of what might have been.

Pomegranate

BOX 6099   ROHNERT PARK   CA 94927

MANHATTAN MEMORIES

South Street, c. 1890
Silver gelatin print

Once the busiest port in the world, New York saw its waterfront
commerce begin to decline in the 1960s as industry moved from
the City, and as container ships began to favor more modern facili-
ties at Elizabeth, New Jersey. Revitalization of the City's abundant
waterfront has been a lively topic in recent years.

BOX 6099   ROHNERT PARK   CA 94927

Pomegranate

MANHATTAN MEMORIES

Public Baths: Swimming Pool, c. 1912
Emil Stopff
Lantern slide

The first public baths in New York City appeared in 1895, when
the state legislature required municipalities with populations of
50,000 or more to build free bathhouses. Most of the baths built
after 1904 also included gymnasiums and swimming pools. The
Tenement House Law of 1901, requiring running water on all
floors, precipitated the decline of public baths.

BOX 6099   ROHNERT PARK   CA 94927

Pomegranate

MANHATTAN MEMORIES

Aerial View of Coney Island, Showing the Elephant Hotel, n.d.
Silver gelatin print

Built in 1882, the Elephant Hotel was an immense tin-clad wooden structure. Its legs housed spiral staircases, a cigar store, and a diorama. Despite the fact that there were just a few rooms in the hotel, visitors flocked to the oddity, taking in the waterfront sights from its observatory.

BOX 6099 ROHNERT PARK CA 94927

Pomegranate

5TH AVE. & 42ND ST.
THE WATER WAS FIRST
LET INTO THIS RESERVOIR
·JULY 4TH 1842·
~DEMOLISHED 1897~

MANHATTAN MEMORIES

Croton Reservoir, n.d.
George P. Hall
Silver gelatin print

Water from the Croton Aqueduct was first let into this imposing
reservoir at 42nd Street and Fifth Avenue on July 4, 1842. It was
demolished in 1897 to make way for the New York Public Library,
which remains on the site today.

BOX 6099   ROHNERT PARK   CA 94927

Pomegranate

MANHATTAN MEMORIES

The Metropolitan Opera House, c.1885
Silver gelatin print
The J. Clarence Davies Collection

The theater that served as the first home of the Metropolitan
Opera opened in 1883 on Broadway and 39th Street. It was built
by members of the growing social elite who were unable to obtain
boxes at the Academy of Music on East 14th Street. Leopold
Stokowski conducted the final performance on April 16, 1966,
on the eve of the building's demolition and the opera's move
to Lincoln Center.

CA 94927

ROHNERT PARK

BOX 6099

Pomegranate

MANHATTAN MEMORIES

National League Opener at Ebbets Field:
Brooklyn Dodgers vs. New York Giants, n.d.
Brown Bros.
Silver gelatin print

Ebbets Field was the fourth and most famous home of the
Brooklyn Dodgers. It opened on April 9, 1913; the Dodgers played
their last game there on September 24, 1957, before their long-
lamented move to Los Angeles. The landmark stadium was
demolished in 1960 to make way for a housing development.

BOX 6099 ROHNERT PARK CA 94927

Pomegranate

MANHATTAN MEMORIES

The Waldorf-Astoria Hotel, n.d.
Silver gelatin print

The Waldorf was erected by William Waldorf Astor in 1893, and John Jacob Astor IV built the Astoria in 1897. The two buildings, both designed by Henry J. Hardenbergh, functioned as one hotel—the largest and most glamorous of the 1890s. It was demolished in 1929, making way for a new landmark, the Empire State Building.

BOX 6099 ROHNERT PARK CA 94927

Pomegranate

Polo Grounds, New York City.
Home of the New York Giants.

MANHATTAN MEMORIES

The Polo Grounds, 1913
Postcard

Built in 1911, the Polo Grounds, at 157th Street and Eighth
Avenue, overlooked the Harlem River and served the New York
Giants from 1911 until 1957; the Yankees from 1913 until 1922;
and the Mets in 1962 and 1963. The legendary ballpark was
demolished in 1964 to make way for a housing project.

BOX 6099   ROHNERT PARK   CA 94927

Pomegranate

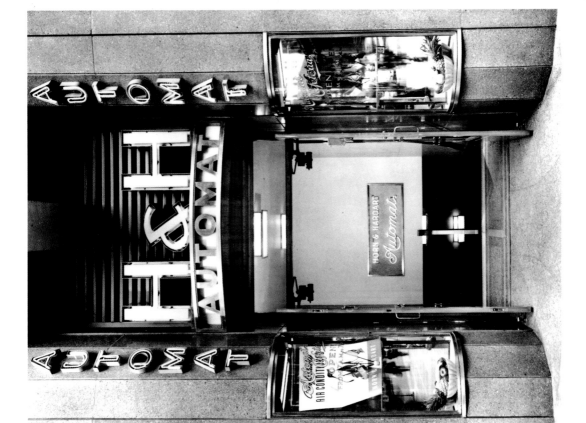

MANHATTAN MEMORIES

Horn & Hardart Automat, n.d.
Wurts Bros.
Silver gelatin print
The Wurts Collection

The world's first Automat opened in New York City in 1912.
These self-service restaurants offered a variety of culinary
delights, such as coffee, soups, entrees, and desserts, behind glass
doors; they were obtained by depositing a coin in a slot. Automats
reached the height of their popularity in the 1940s and 1950s,
but began to decline in the 1970s with the advent of fast-food
restaurants. The last Automat closed on April 8, 1991.

BOX 6099 ROHNERT PARK CA 94927

Pomegranate

MANHATTAN MEMORIES

Woolworth's Lunch Counter, n.d.
Wurts Bros.
Silver gelatin print
The Wurts Collection

The first Woolworth's "five and ten" store in New York City
opened in 1896 at 17th Street and Sixth Avenue. The ubiquitous
lunch counter was a familiar sight to New Yorkers, and indeed to
all Americans.

BOX 6099   ROHNERT PARK   CA 94927

Pomegranate

MANHATTAN MEMORIES

Coney Island: Parachute Jump in Steeplechase Park, n.d.
New York Convention and Visitors Bureau

In 1941, the 250-foot-high Life Savers Corporation Parachute
Tower was salvaged from the 1939 New York World's Fair and
relocated to Coney Island's Steeplechase Park, where it thrilled
riders for 28 years. Though inactive, the tapered steel structure
remains a visible and registered landmark.

BOX 6099   ROHNERT PARK   CA 94927

Pomegranate

MANHATTAN MEMORIES

Newsboys, c. 1900
Silver gelatin print

"Newsies" at the turn of the century paid cash for an armload
of papers and ate the loss if they failed to sell them. In order to
collect early-morning editions fresh off the press, they had to
arrive at newspaper offices hours before dawn.

BOX 6099   ROHNERT PARK   CA 94927

Pomegranate

MANHATTAN MEMORIES

Organ Grinder with Monkey, 1929
Rudolph Simmon
Gift of Mrs. Kay Simmon Blumberg

Popular in the early twentieth century, these street musicians
carried an organ called a "hurdy-gurdy" that was played by turning
a crank. Organ grinders were often accompanied by monkeys that
collected coins from spectators.

BOX 6099   ROHNERT PARK   CA 94927

Pomegranate

MANHATTAN MEMORIES

West 42nd Street, 1984
Andreas Feininger
Gift of Mr. Andreas Feininger

Times Square was infamous for its seedy nightlife and thriving pornography industry. A 1990s revitalization project brought mainstream retailers and lawsuits that forced out the notorious tenants of the neighborhood, radically altering the image of Times Square.

BOX 6099   ROHNERT PARK   CA 94927

Pomegranate

MANHATTAN MEMORIES

Traffic Tower at Fifth Avenue and 34th Street, 1930s
Silver gelatin print
Gift of Frederic Lewis

The first electric traffic signals for New York City were erected in 1919 along Fifth Avenue. An operator inside the windowed booth directed competing flows of traffic by manually adjusting the red, green, and amber lights. To the right, the B. Altman & Co. department store—now a site of the City University of New York and the New York Public Library—stands in its retail heyday.

BOX 6099   ROHNERT PARK   CA 94927

Pomegranate

MANHATTAN MEMORIES

Children's Penny Merry-Go-Round, 1926
Silver gelatin print
Gift of Miss Flora Jo Bergstrom

Throughout New York's history, street entertainers have provided
various forms of amusement for children and adults alike.
Merry-go-rounds, or carousels, were common in the early
twentieth century.

BOX 6099   ROHNERT PARK   CA 94927

Pomegranate